The Cajun Fisherman and His Wife

Connie Collins Morgan
Illustrated by Herb Leonhard

PELICAN PUBLISHING COMPANY
GRETNA 2018

*The word "Pelican" and the depiction of a pelican are
trademarks of Pelican Publishing Company, Inc., and are
registered in the U.S. Patent and Trademark Office.*

Library of Congress Cataloging-in-Publication Data

Names: Morgan, Connie Collins, author. | Leonhard, Herb, illustrator.
Title: The Cajun fisherman and his wife / by Connie Collins Morgan ;
    illustrated by Herb Leonhard.
Other titles: Fisherman and his wife. English.
Description: Gretna : Pelican Publishing Company, 2018. | Summary: When Cajun
    fisherman Paul encounters an enchanted, wish-granting sac-a-lait, his
    wife, Paulette, wishes for many things, including a crawfish pot and the
    title of Mardi Gras queen. Includes glossary.
Identifiers: LCCN 2017036719| ISBN 9781455623662 (hardcover : alk. paper) |
    ISBN 9781455623679 (ebook)
Subjects: | CYAC: Fairy tales. | Folklore—Germany.
Classification: LCC PZ8.M8213 Caj 2018 | DDC 398.2 [E] —dc23 LC record
available at https://lccn.loc.gov/2017036719

Printed in China

Published by Pelican Publishing Company, Inc.
1000 Burmaster Street, Gretna, Louisiana 70053

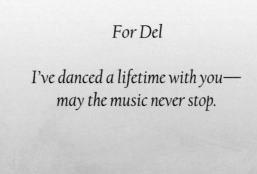

For Del

I've danced a lifetime with you—
may the music never stop.

In a small house nestled beneath a canopy of towering oaks, there lived a fisherman and his wife. Paul and Paulette led a simple life, where each day was the same as the day before.

One morning before the sun awoke, Paul went down to the bayou. The white egret croaked a good morning to the fisherman while he sat in his pirogue and fished. As the sun peeked through the cypress trees, Paul's float plunged beneath the murky waters.

He yanked and he pulled and he pulled and he yanked. "There ain't no way you gettin' away from me, boy."

A bullfrog, stunned by the struggle, bellowed,

"The fish was a-splashin' as Paul went a-crashin'
down to the bottom of the boat."

Kerplunk!

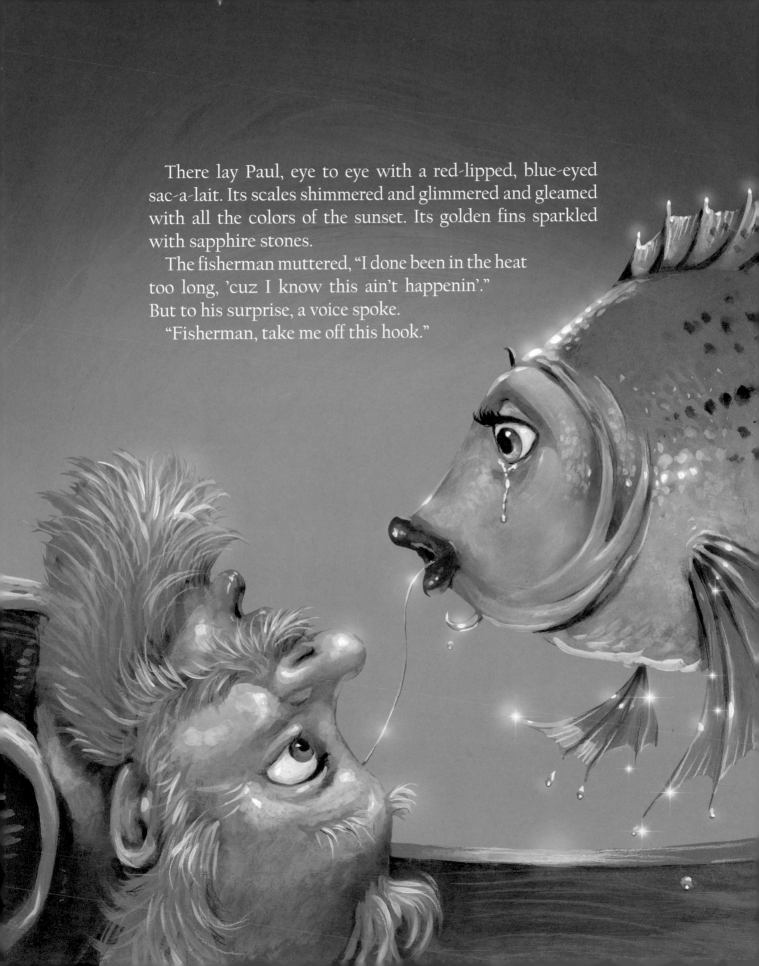

There lay Paul, eye to eye with a red-lipped, blue-eyed sac-a-lait. Its scales shimmered and glimmered and gleamed with all the colors of the sunset. Its golden fins sparkled with sapphire stones.

The fisherman muttered, "I done been in the heat too long, 'cuz I know this ain't happenin'." But to his surprise, a voice spoke.

"Fisherman, take me off this hook."

Paul threw his pole into the air. *"Bon Dieu,* a talkin' fish!"

The sac-a-lait flipped and flapped, pleading for its freedom. "Don't eat me, Fisherman!"

"You ain't got to worry about that," said Paul, "'cuz I don't eat talkin' fish!"

"But I am not a fish!" the sac-a-lait cried. "The evil swamp queen cast a spell on me. Let me go, and I will grant any wishes that you want."

The sac-a-lait could tell that Paul didn't believe her, so she tossed and turned, and dozens of crawfish jumped into his pirogue.

Paul's eyes lit up. "Paulette ain't never gonna believe this!"
He unhooked the fish and tossed her into the bayou. The
sac-a-lait disappeared and Paul returned home to his wife.

That evening, Paul told Paulette about the talking sac-a-lait that granted wishes. "*Mais*, Paul, why you didn't ask that fish for a pot to boil them crawfish?" She stomped her foot. "Go tell that sac-a-lait to give me a crawfish pot."

When Paul returned to the bayou, the sweltering sun beat down upon him. "Sac-a-lait!" he called. A glow of shimmering gold spiraled into the air.

A brown owl, amazed by the golden luster, hooted,

"The fish was a-splashin' as Paul went a-crashin' down to the bottom of the boat."

Kerplunk!

The red-lipped, blue-eyed sac-a-lait landed on top of Paul.
"What do you want, Fisherman?"

"Sac-a-lait, my wife wants one of them crawfish pots."
"Go home, Fisherman. Your wife has her pot."

That night Paul and Paulette feasted until they could eat no more. Paulette danced beneath the moonlight to the sound of accordion runs. Her musical laughter brought a whisper of joy into Paul's life. "Now you look happy," he said.

"For now," Paulette replied.
And nothing more was said.

As days turned into weeks, Paul thought his wife was happy. But Paulette mumbled and grumbled. "Paul! I done got me an idea. I gonna open me one of them gumbo shops in our home."

Paul shook his head. "Why you wanna do somethin' like that?"

"My cookin' will be the best tastin' on the bayou. Go tell that fish what I want."

The sizzling rays of the sun blinded Paul when he returned to the bayou. "Sac-a-lait!" he called. The fish soared above the bayou, splashing water from her sapphire fins.
A gator, basking in the sun, growled,

"The fish was a-splashin' as Paul went a-crashin' down to the bottom of the boat."

Kerplunk!

There lay Paul with Ol' Ruby Lips.

"What does your wife want now?" asked the fish.

"She wants her cookin' to be the best tastin' on the bayou."

"Go home, Fisherman," said the sac-a-lait. "Your wife is known as the best cook around."

When Paul arrived, people lined the banks of the bayou—the Boudreauxs, the Thibodeauxs, and the Arceneauxs. Everyone raved about Paulette's gumbo.

"Are you happy?" Paul asked.

"For now," she answered. And nothing more was said.

As weeks turned into months, Paul thought his wife seemed satisfied. But Paulette moaned and groaned. "Mais, I can't feed the people in this little house no more. I need one of them big homes on the other side of the bayou where the rich folk live."

Paul shook his head. "We fine in this house, Paulette." But when his wife wailed louder, he went back to the bayou.

The sun reached down and singed every blade of grass that covered the water's edge. Paul dug his push-pole into the bottom of the bayou and called, "Sac-a-lait!" The blue-eyed fish exploded from the water, creating a spectacular show of spins and turns.

A cottonmouth, slithering by, hissed,

"The fish was a-splashin' as Paul went a-crashin' down to the bottom of the boat."

Kerplunk!

"Sac-a-lait! My wife wants one of them big homes on the other side of the bayou where the rich folk live."

"Go home, Fisherman. Your wife lives among the wealthy in a large home."

When Paul arrived, Paulette greeted him from the balcony. "There ain't no house bigger than this on the bayou," she said.

Paul pleaded, "Tell me you happy."

"For now," she answered. And nothing more was said.

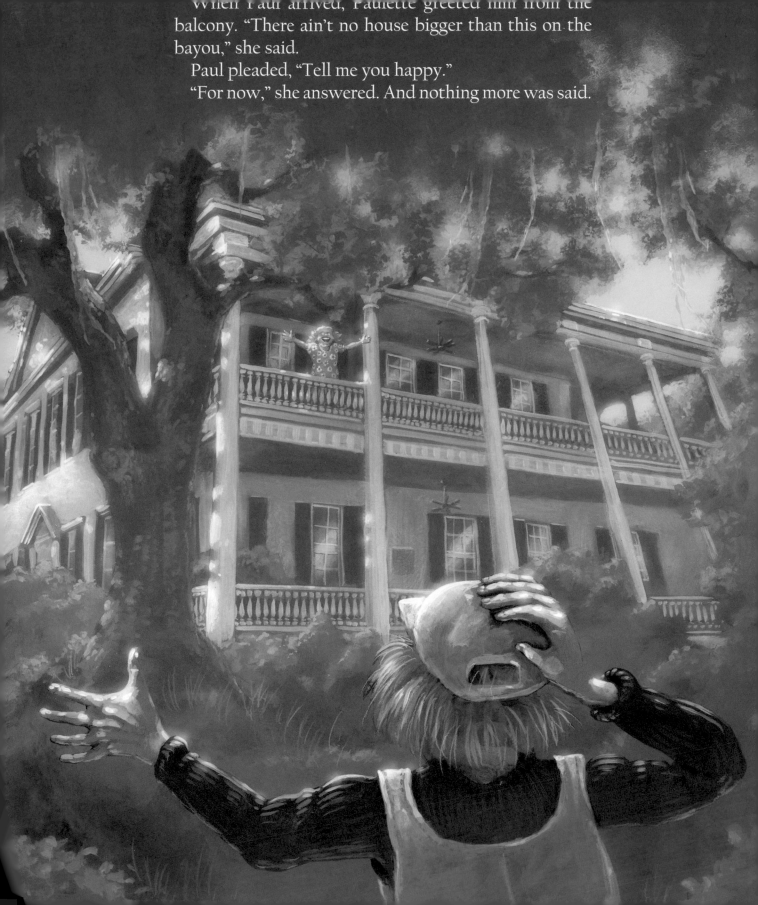

As months turned into years, Paul believed that his wife was finally content. Then one day, Paulette slammed the door, crying. "Paul! Marie said I ain't never gonna be queen of the Mardi Gras Ball. She tol' me I'm jus' not the queenly type."

Paul hugged his wife. **"Mais,** that's nothin' to cry about. You always gonna be my queen."

Paulette wailed louder. "Go tell that fish to make me queen of the Mardi Gras Ball!"

Paul reluctantly returned to the bayou. The banks cracked under the sun's fury. "Sac-a-lait!" called the fisherman.

The fish surfaced at the water's edge. "What does your wife want now?"

"Paulette wants to be queen of the Mardi Gras Ball!"

"No, Fisherman. Your wife cannot be queen. Go home."
"But Paulette ain't gonna be happy," said Paul.
"Your wife's wishes will not bring her happiness.
Go home, Fisherman. You will find Paulette as
she was before you ever knew me."

Paul understood the sac-a-lait's wisdom. As he knelt by the fish, stroking her golden fins, the sac-a-lait spoke for the last time. "May I grant one final wish to a kindhearted fisherman?"

"I only have one wish," said Paul, "one unspoken wish."
"Consider it granted," replied the sac-a-lait.

"In the mornin', the swamp queen will meet you here," said Paul. "Then, you will know my wish."

Paul returned to his small house beneath the towering oaks.

Never again did he see the talking sac-a-lait. Life on the bayou was like he once knew it. And Paulette was happy. She wasn't upset when she heard about the Mardi Gras Ball from the rich folks on the bayou. She even smiled when they raved about the new Mardi Gras queen.

"Paulette," they rambled, "she was like none we had ever seen! Her eyes were like the deepest blues of the ocean, and her lips were ruby red. Her gown shimmered and glimmered and gleamed with all the colors of the sunset. And around her neck was a golden chain with sapphire stones."

Paul smiled. His eyes moistened.
And nothing more was said.

Author's Note

Some of the best-known works of literature are the folktales of Jacob and Wilhelm Grimm. The Brothers Grimm wrote over two hundred short stories and fairy tales that children have read around the world.

The Cajun Fisherman and His Wife is based on the Brothers Grimm story of a kindhearted fisherman who catches a magical fish, and his wife's unbridled greed that leads to discontentment. This retelling celebrates the rich culture of the Cajun people and the value they place on the simple and good things in life.

Glossary

bayou (BY-yoo)—A slow-moving, swampy body of water.

Bon Dieu **(bon dyoo)**—A French expression that literally means "good God" but is more often used as "good heavens."

Cajun (KAY-jun)—A member of a group of people in south Louisiana who descended from exiled French-Canadian settlers known as Acadians.

cottonmouth or water moccasin—A snake that lives in marshy lowlands and has a potentially deadly bite. It grows up to four feet long and is blackish in color.

crawfish—A small freshwater shellfish that resembles a lobster.

gumbo—A kind of soup that includes okra, chicken, sausage, or seafood. The word "gumbo" comes from West Africa and means "okra."

mais **(may)**—A French word that literally means "but." It is more often used as "yes" or "well, yeah."

Mardi Gras (MAHR-dee grah)—Literally, French for "Fat Tuesday." This festival takes place the day before Lent begins and involves parades, costumes, and lots of food.

pirogue (PEE-rogh)—A narrow, flat canoe that is pushed through a bayou or swamp with a push-pole.

push-pole—A long pole used for pushing a boat through water.

sac-a-lait (SAK-uh-lay)—A freshwater sunfish (crappie) that is about twelve inches long, weighing one to two pounds.

white egret (EE-gret)—A large bird that lives in marshes and can have a wingspan up to fifty inches.